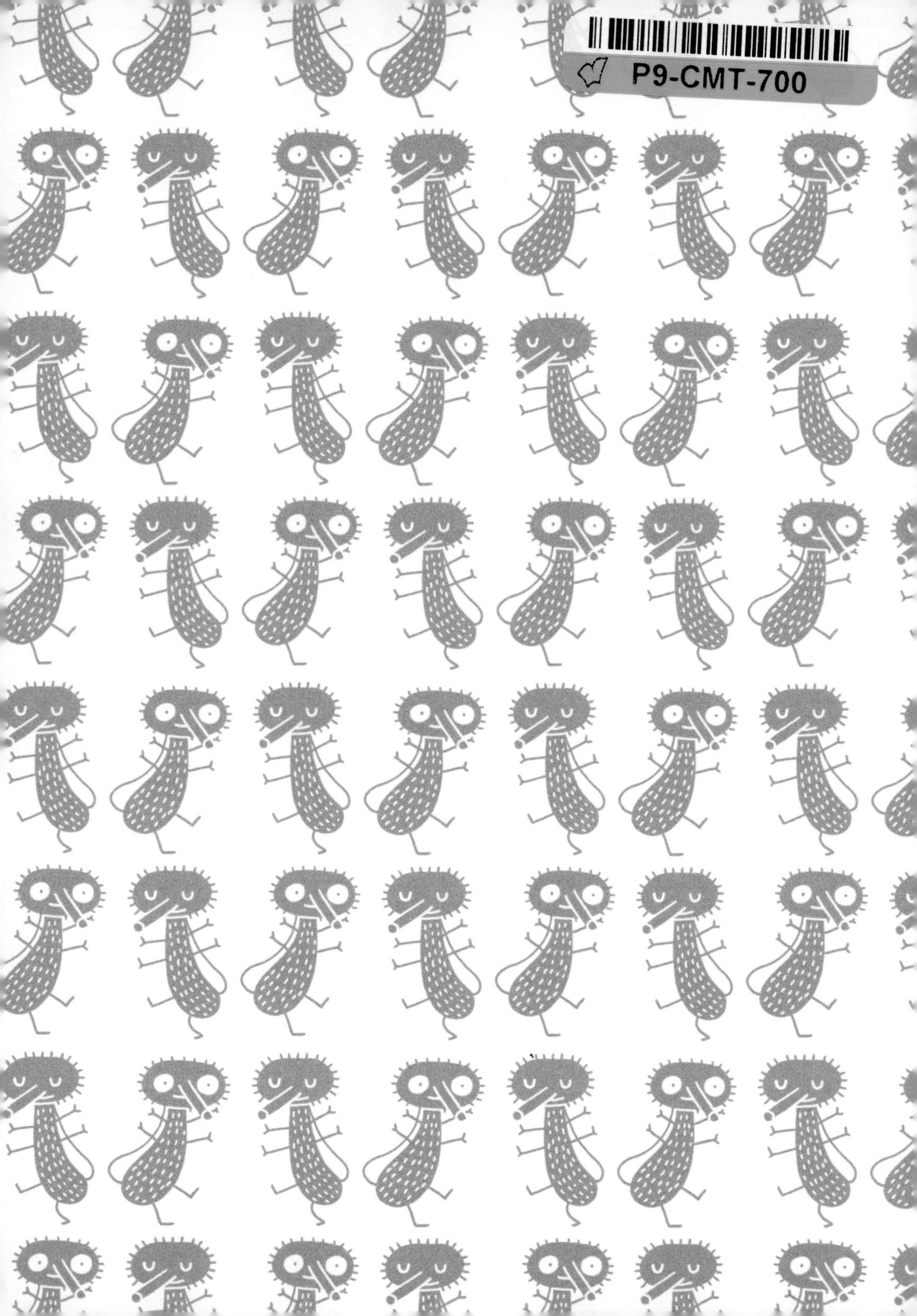

THE FLY

For Sophie,
my little fruit fly

Originally published as *La mouche* by Les éditions de la courte échelle inc.

Copyright © 2014 Elise Gravel
Copyright for the French edition: Elise Gravel and Les éditions de la courte échelle inc., 2012

Published in Canada by Tundra Books, a division of Random House of Canada Limited,
One Toronto Street, Suite 300, Toronto, Ontario M5C 2V6

Published in the United States by Tundra Books of Northern New York,
P.O. Box 1030, Plattsburgh, New York 12901

Library of Congress Control Number: 2013940757

Library and Archives Canada Cataloguing in Publication

Gravel, Elise
[Mouche. English]
      The fly / written and illustrated by Elise Gravel.

(Disgusting critters)
Translation of: La mouche.
Issued in print and electronic formats.
ISBN 978-1-77049-636-1 (pbk.).—ISBN 978-1-77049-638-5 (epub)

      I. Flies—Juvenile literature. I. Title. II. Title: Mouche. English.

QL533.2.G7213 2014   j595.77   C2013-903533-8

English edition edited by Samantha Swenson
Designed by Elise Gravel and Tundra Books
The artwork in this book was rendered digitally.

www.tundrabooks.com

Printed and bound in China

5 6 7 8   21 20 19 18

Elise Gravel

THE FLY

Tundra Books

Let me introduce you
to a very special guy.

HERE'S

THE FLY.

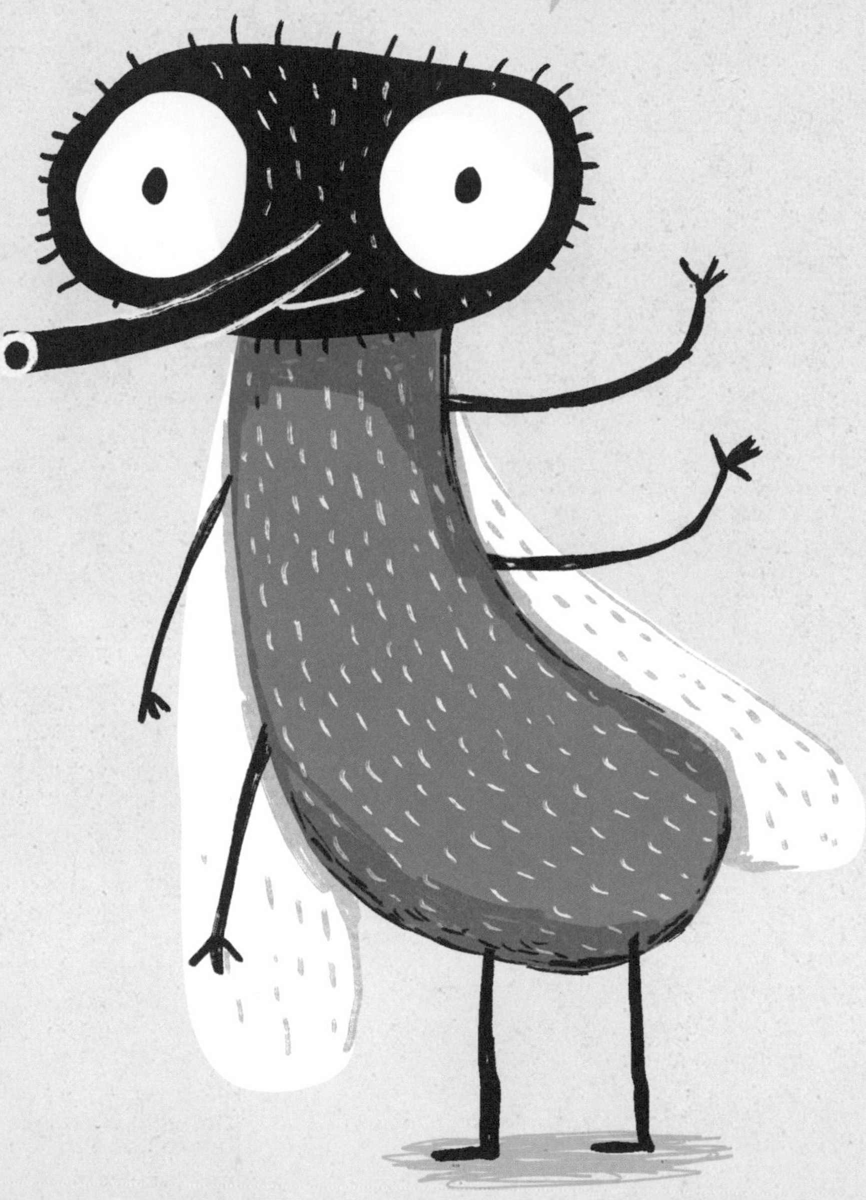
Hey there!

There are more than

100,000

SPECIES OF FLIES

in the world.

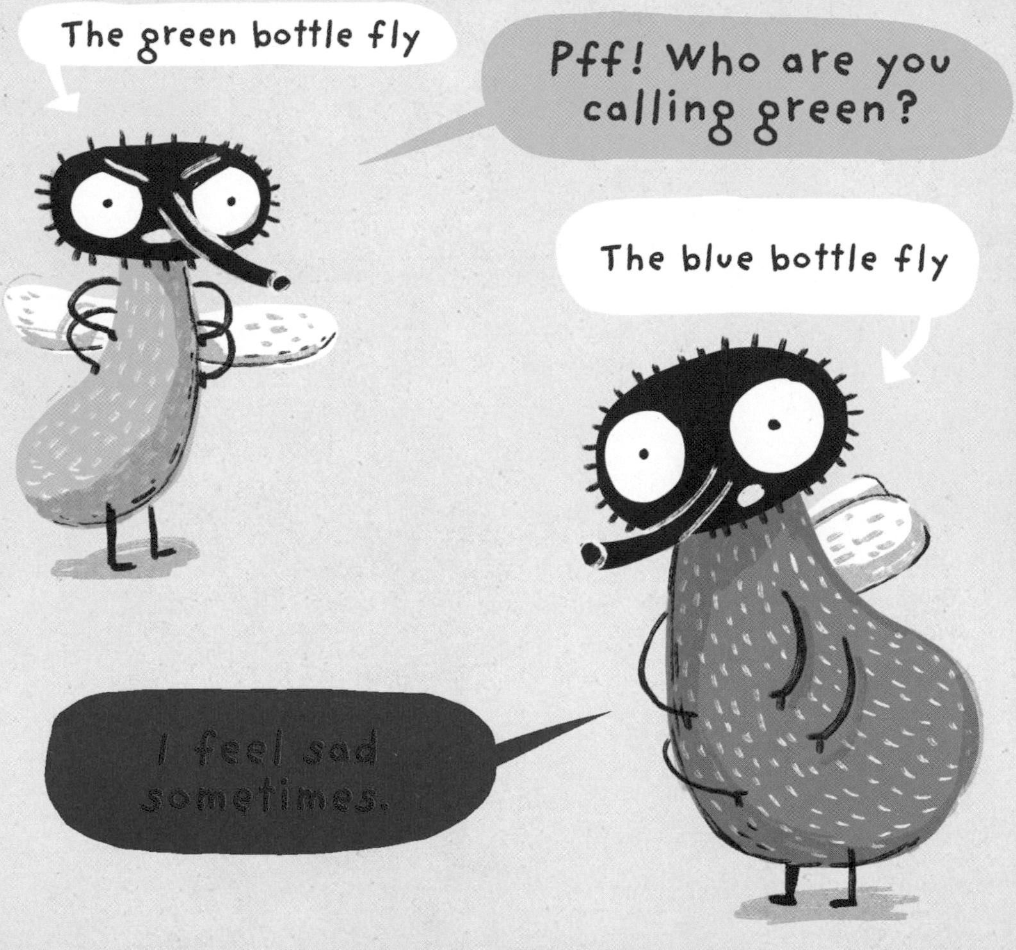
The green bottle fly
Pff! Who are you calling green?
The blue bottle fly
I feel sad sometimes.

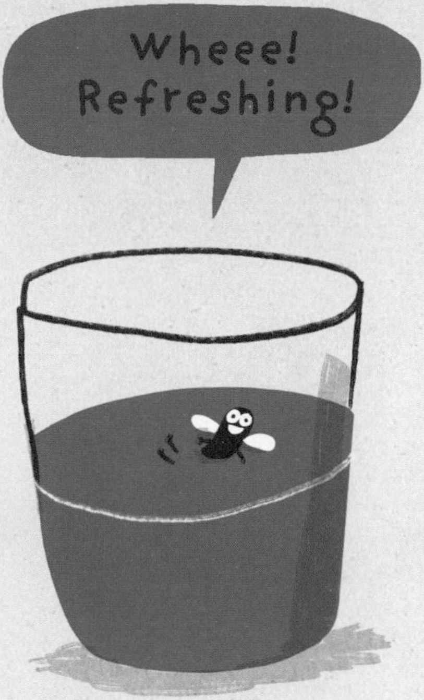
Wheee!
Refreshing!

The fruit fly

Also known as
Drosophila.

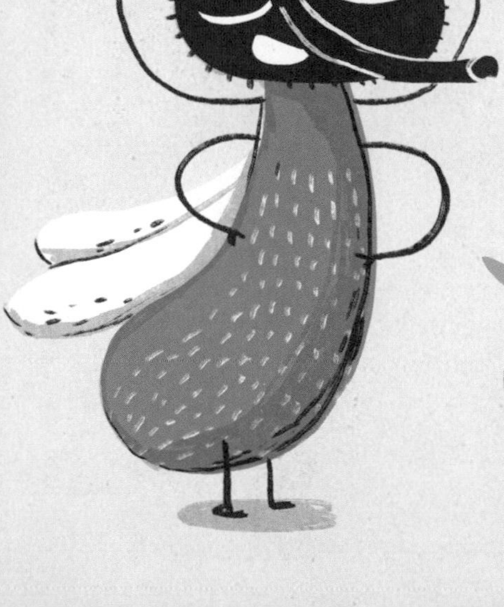

The housefly

He's the hero
of this book.

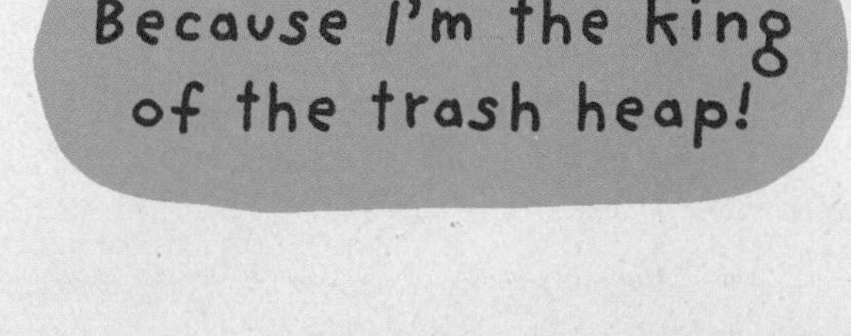
Because I'm the king
of the trash heap!

The housefly is a member of the

MUSCIDAE FAMILY.

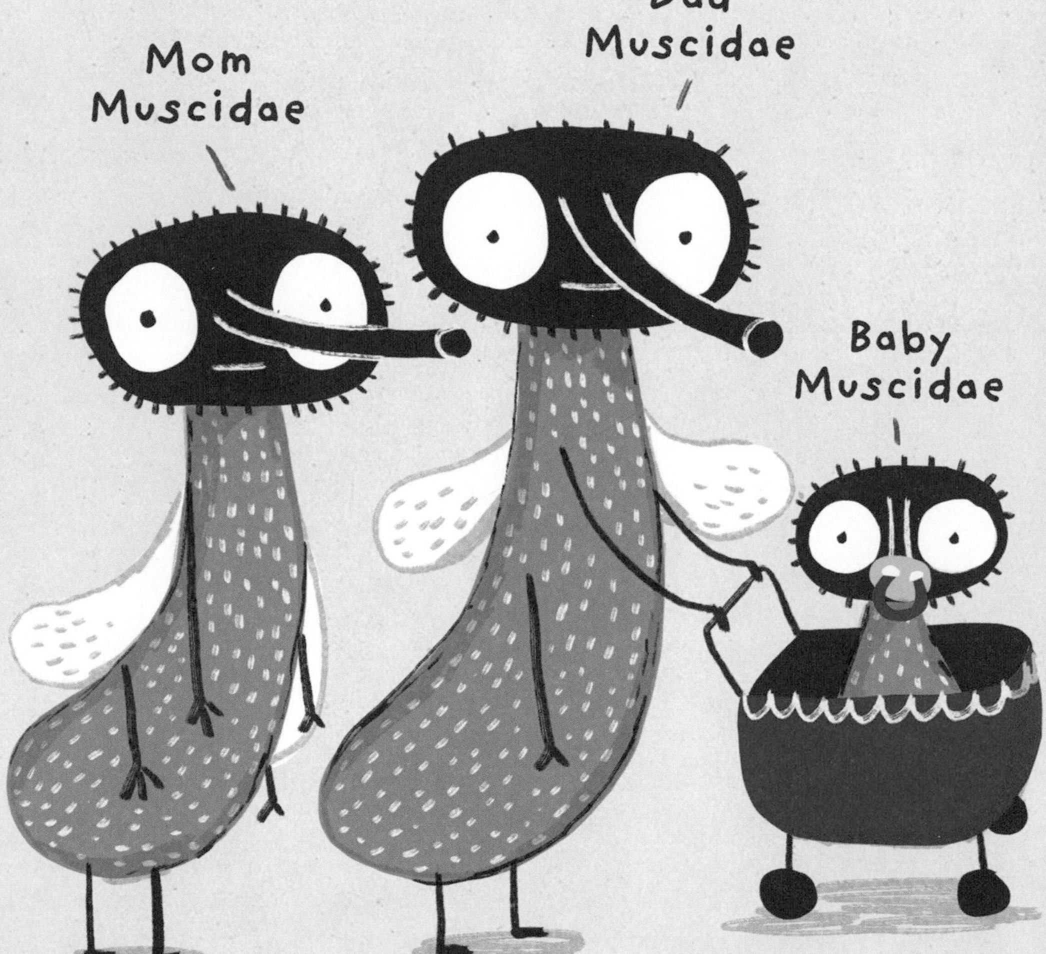
Mom Muscidae
Dad Muscidae
Baby Muscidae

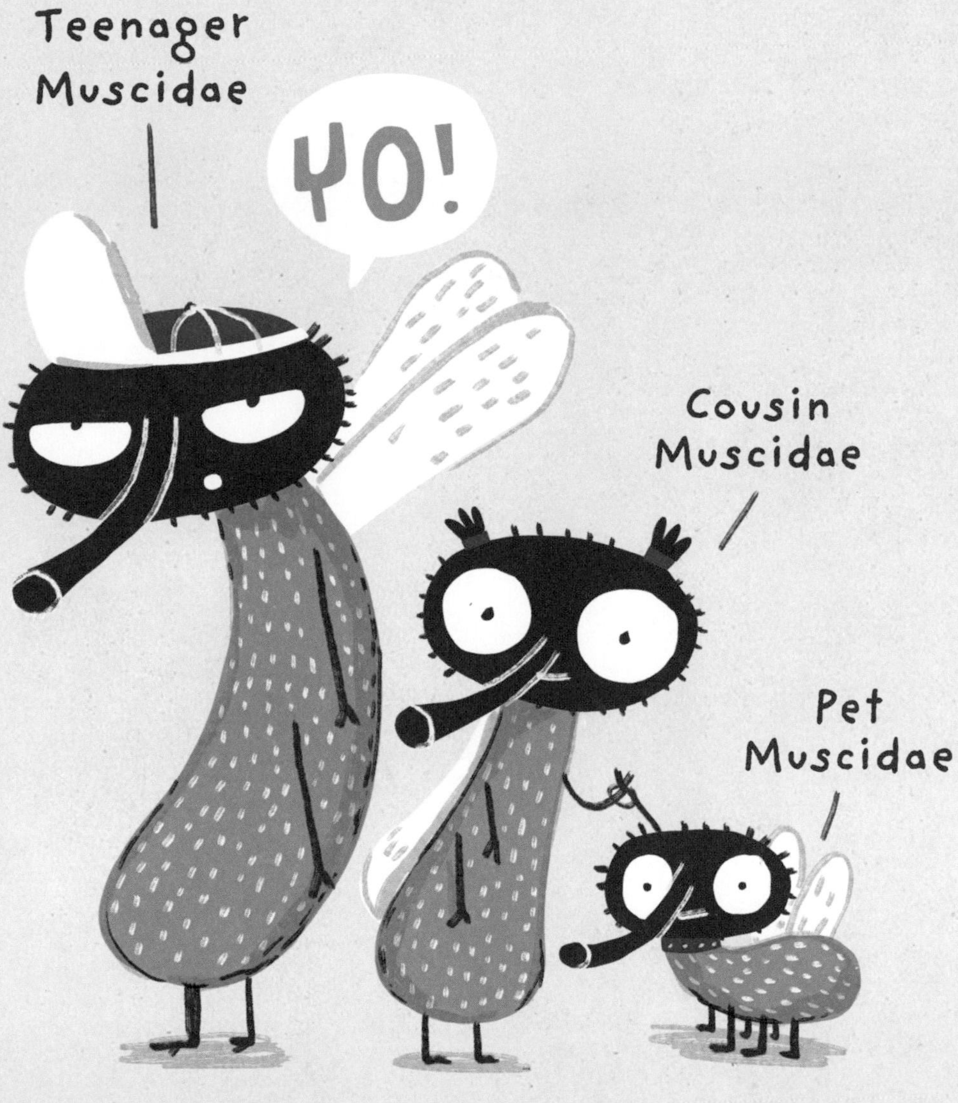
Teenager Muscidae
YO!
Cousin Muscidae
Pet Muscidae

We don't call him the

HOUSEFLY

because he's a pet, like a dog or cat, but because he likes to get inside our

HOUSES.

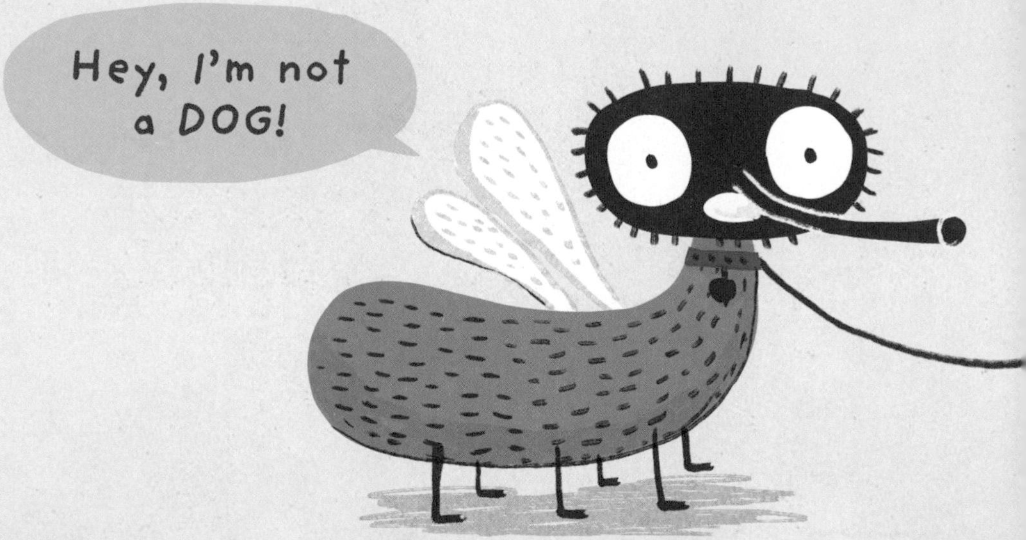
Hey, I'm not a DOG!

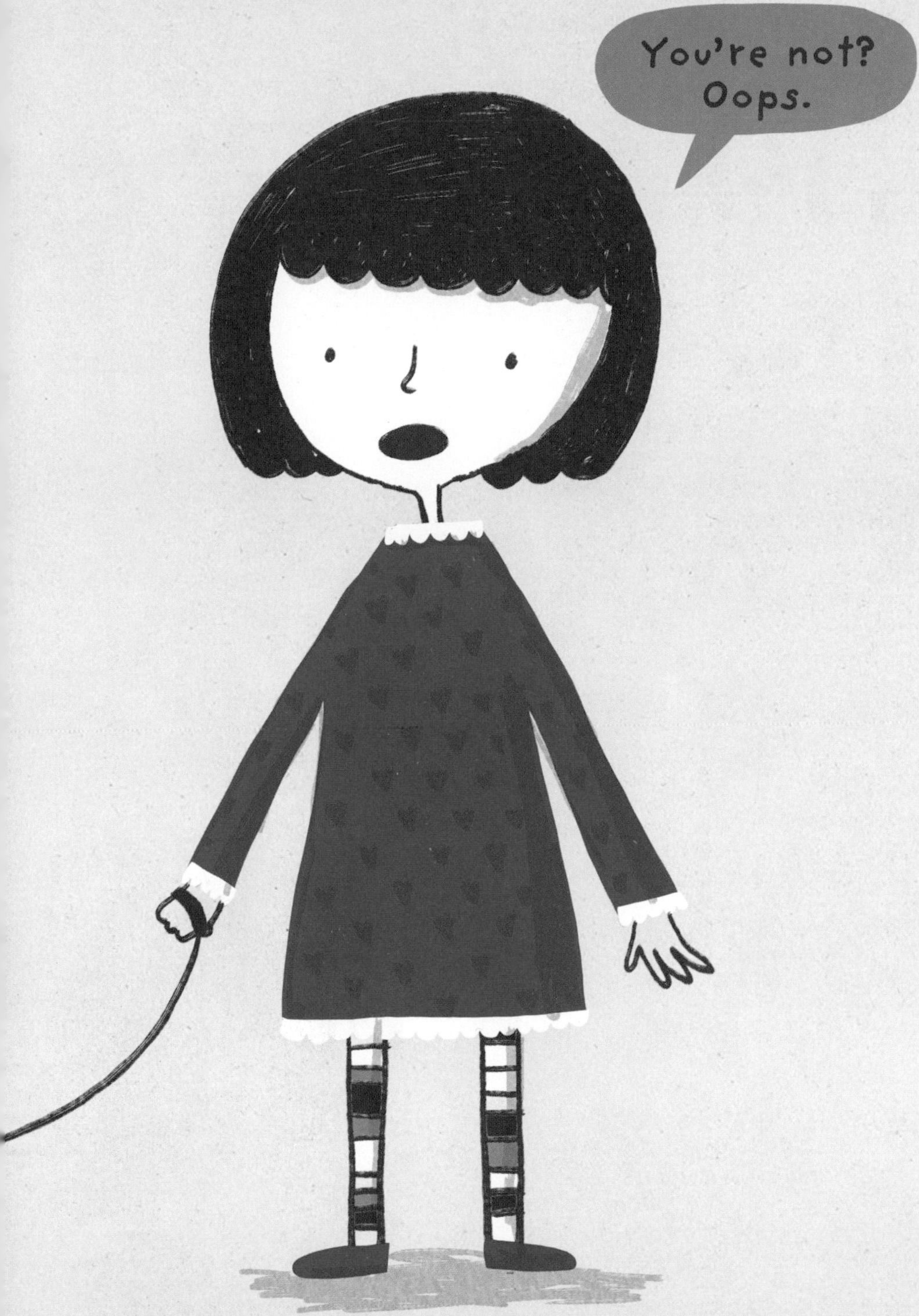
You're not? Oops.

The housefly is found in every country in the world. Houseflies like humans because we offer them a warm place to live and lots of

GARBAGE TO EAT.

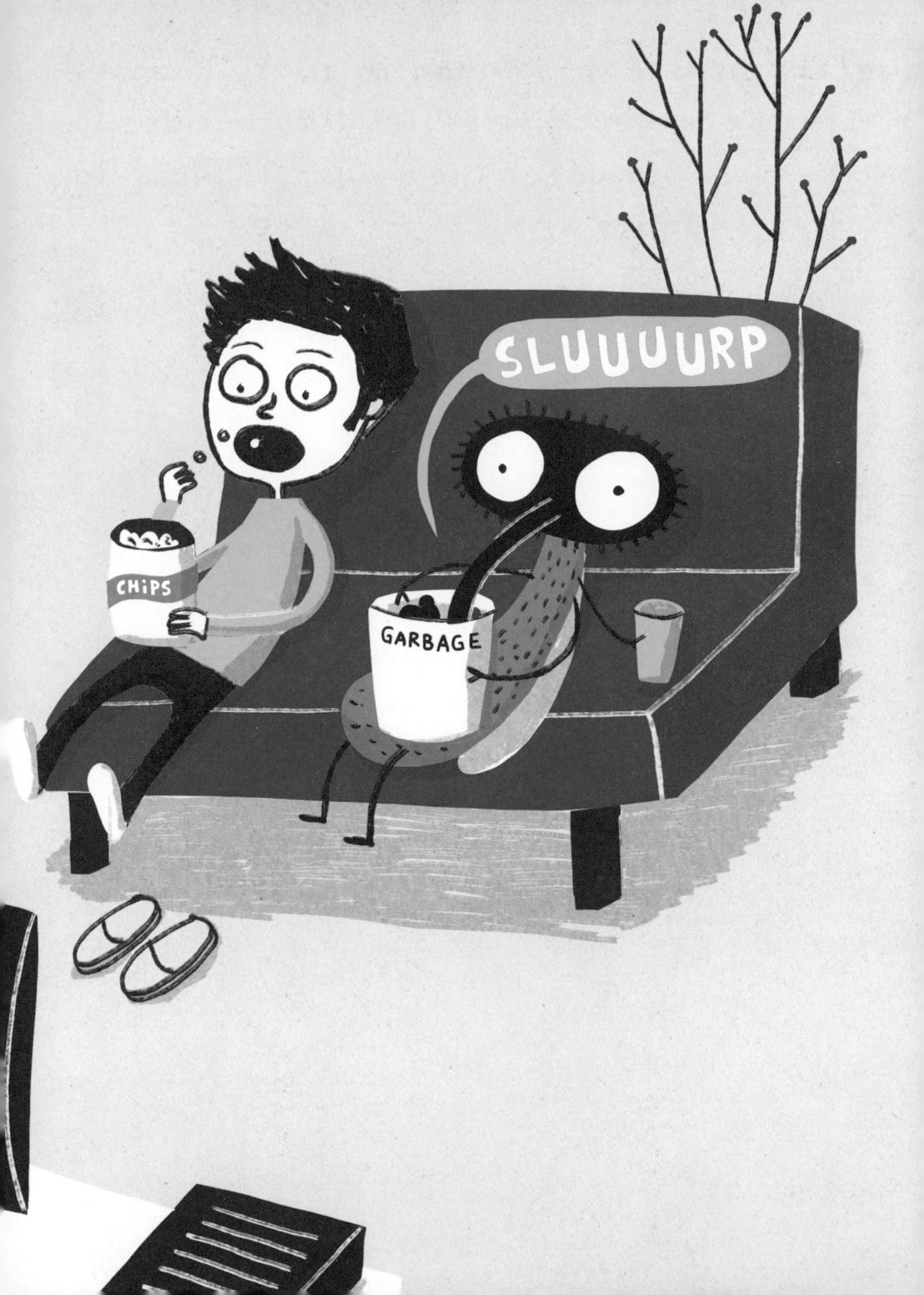
SLUUUURP
CHiPS
GARBAGE

The housefly is gray, with black stripes on his back, and his body is

COVERED WITH HAIR.

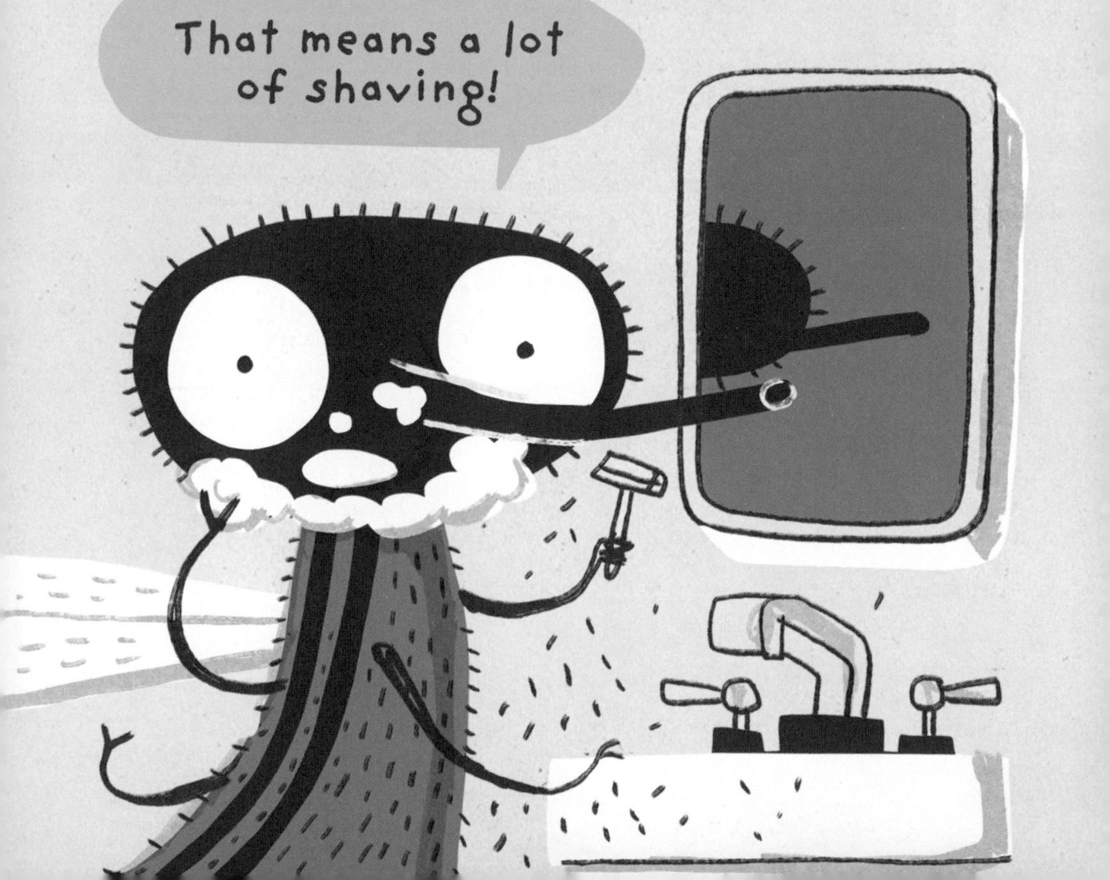
That means a lot of shaving!

The housefly measures from 0.2 to 0.3 inches (5 to 8 millimeters) long. The female is slightly bigger than the male.

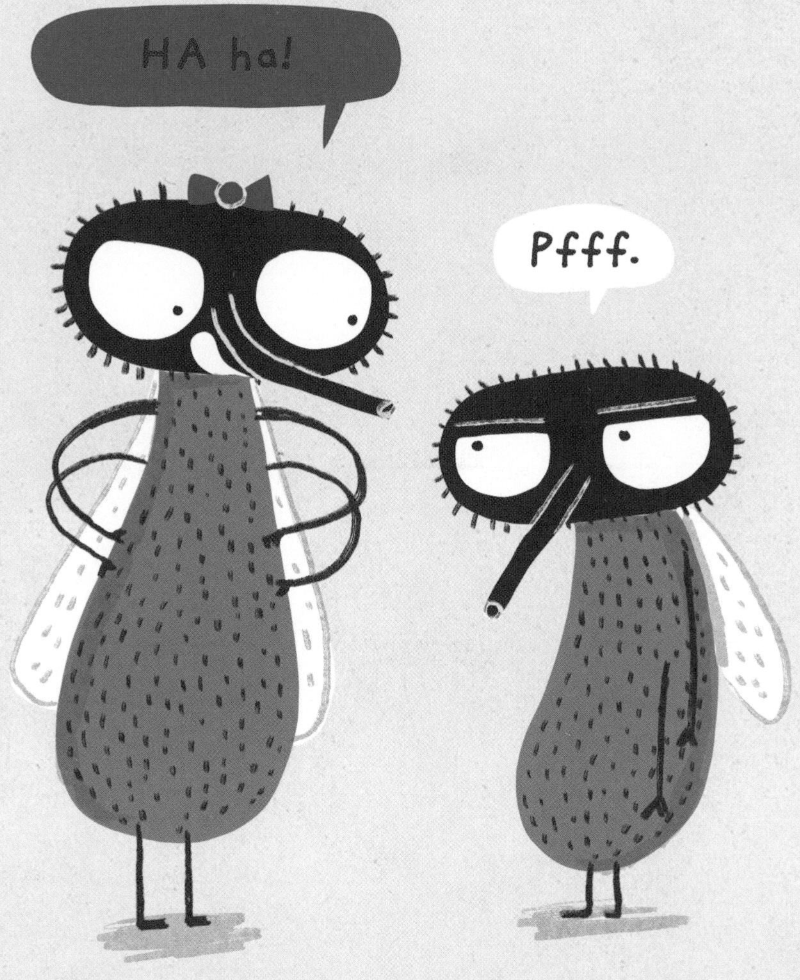
HA ha!
Pfff.

The housefly's eyes are red and have many tiny flat surfaces that allow him to see in all directions at the same time.

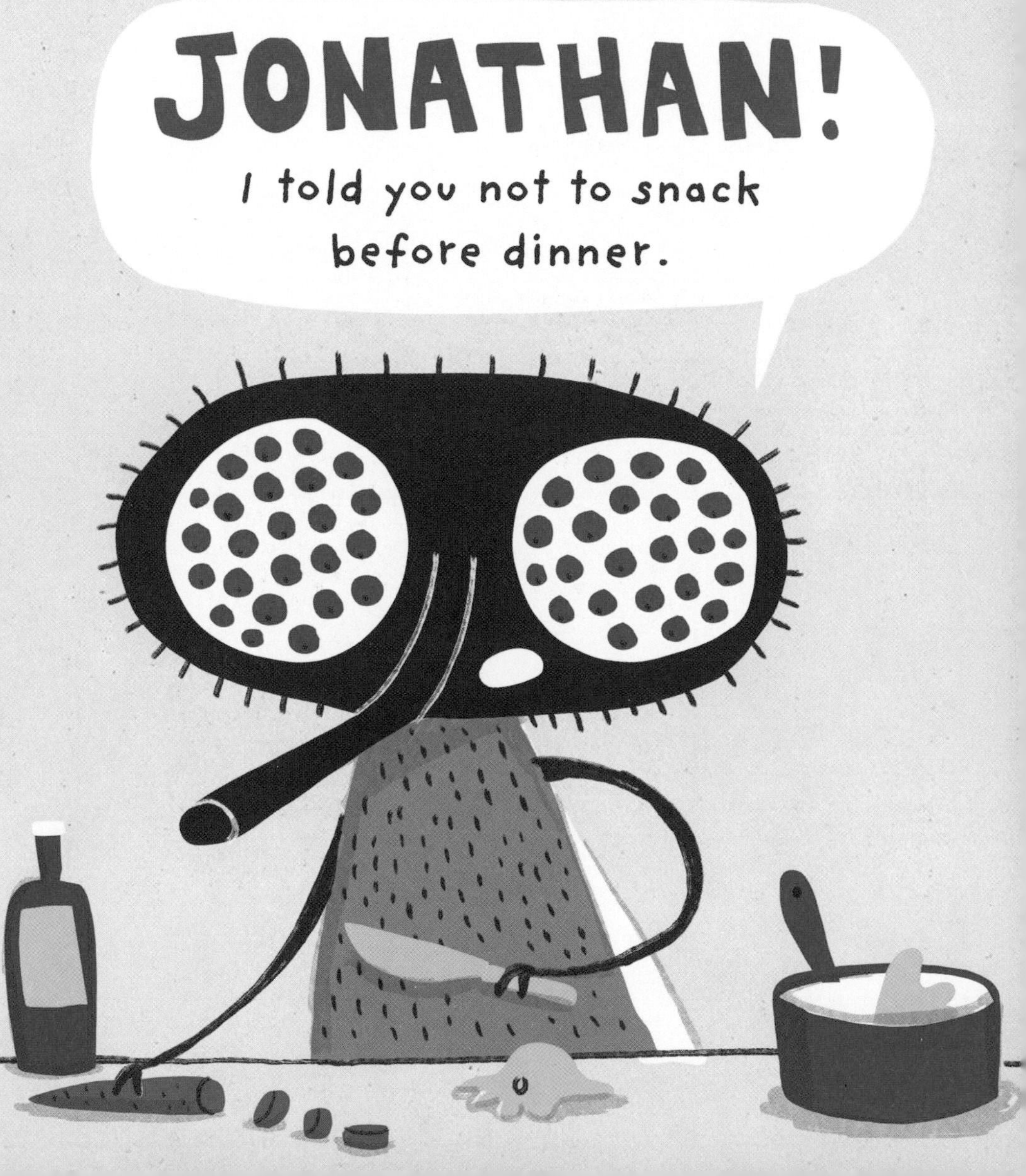
JONATHAN!
I told you not to snack before dinner.

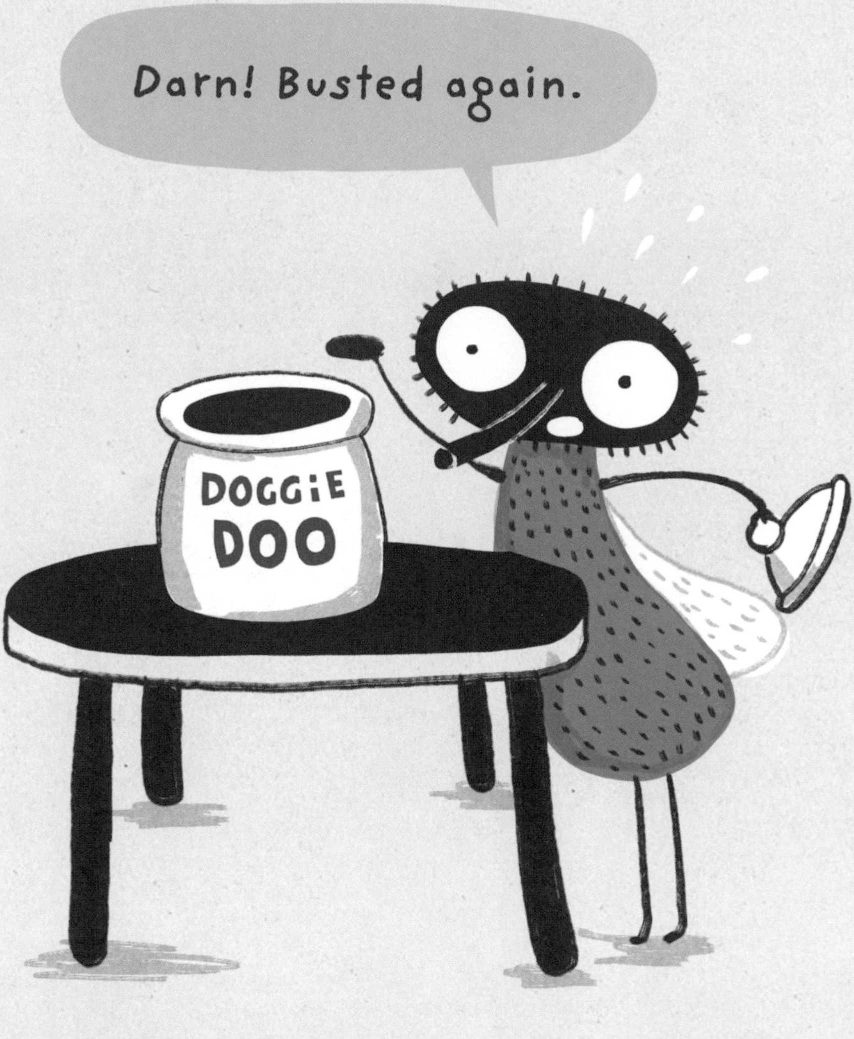
Darn! Busted again.
DOGGiE DOO

Thanks to little

BUBBLES OF LIQUID

at the ends of his feet, the housefly
can walk on walls or even on the

CEILING.

It's pretty cool,
but it's not easy to
play soccer up here.

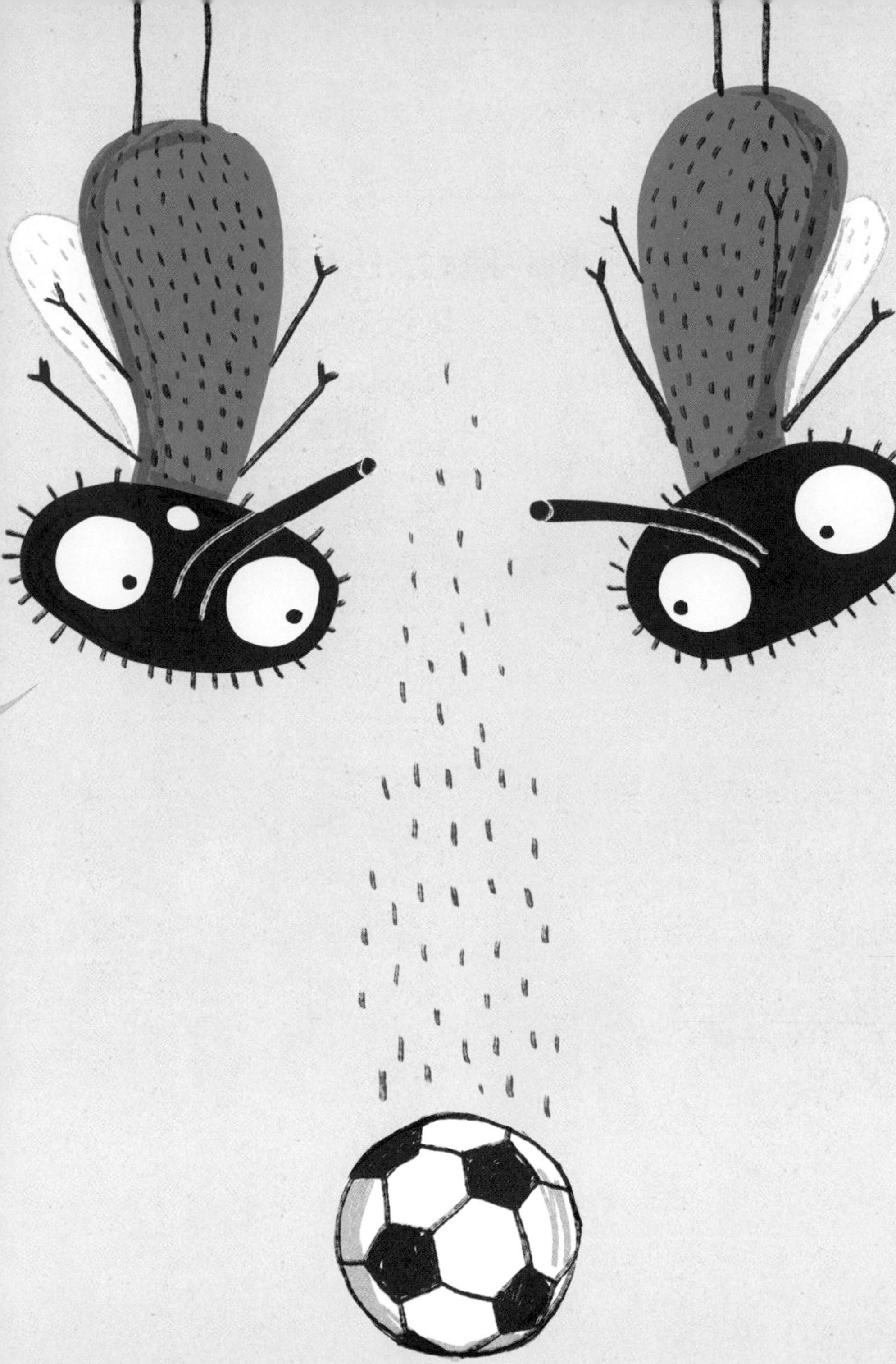

The housefly uses his tube-shaped mouth to suck up his food. He can only eat

LIQUID FOODS, or just LIQUID,

so he spits or vomits a bit of digestive fluid on his meal to soften it.

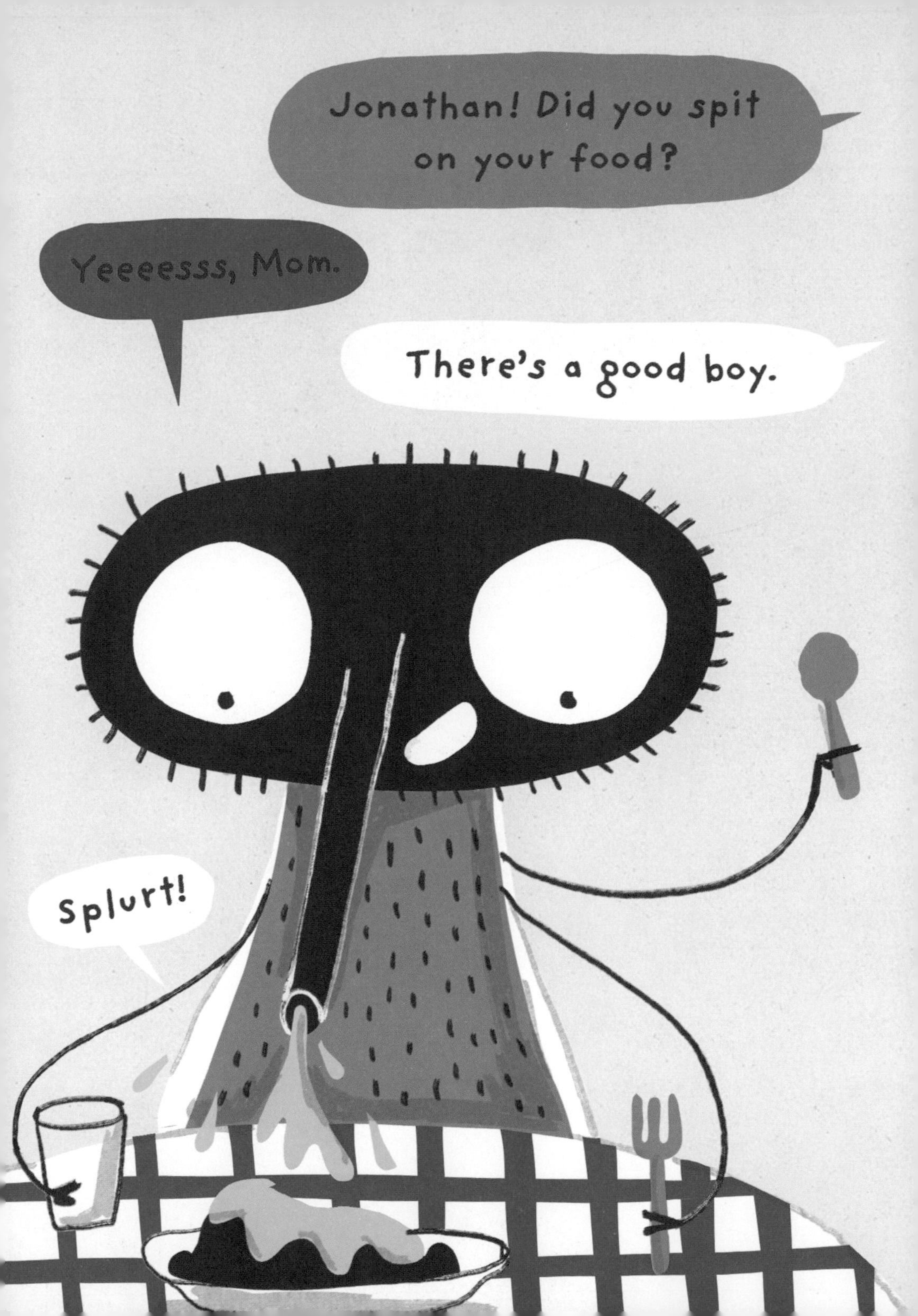
Jonathan! Did you spit on your food?
Yeeeesss, Mom.
There's a good boy.
Splurt!

The fly has really

DISGUSTING TASTE IN FOOD.

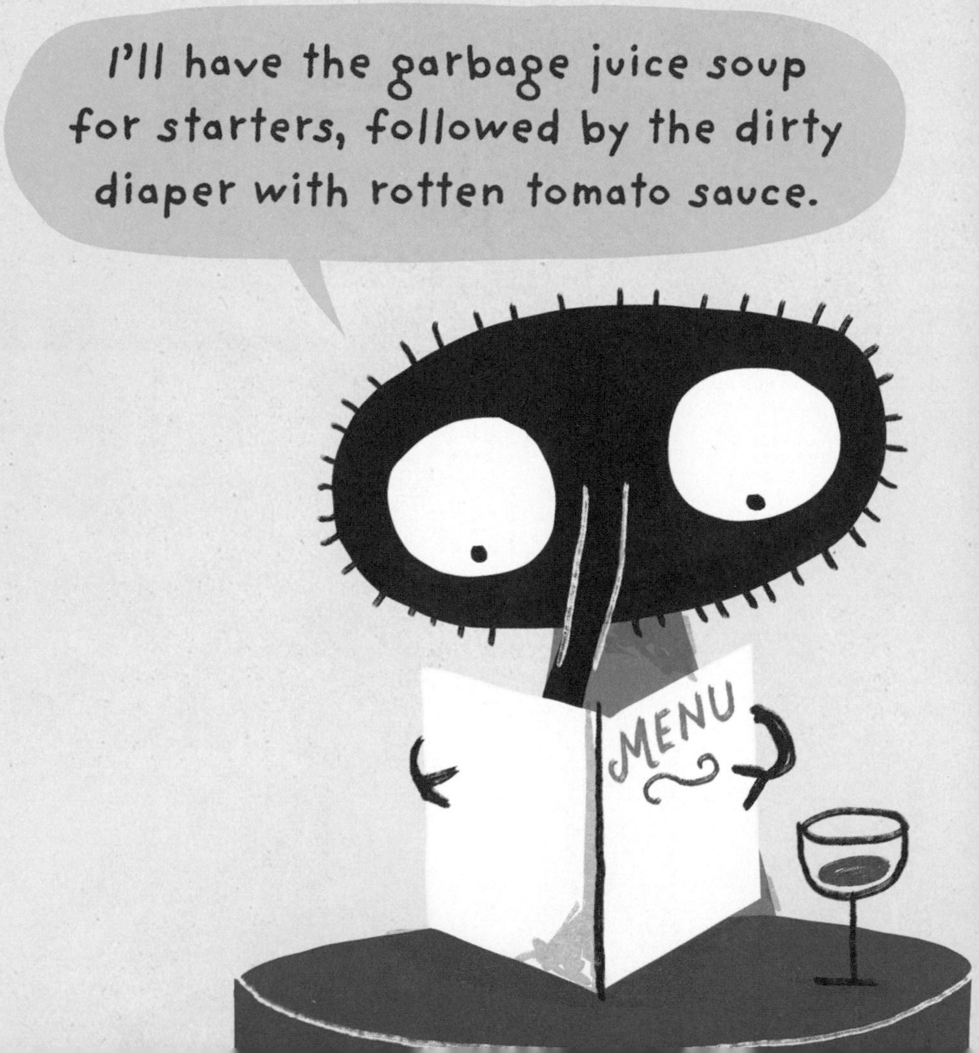
I'll have the garbage juice soup for starters, followed by the dirty diaper with rotten tomato sauce.
MENU

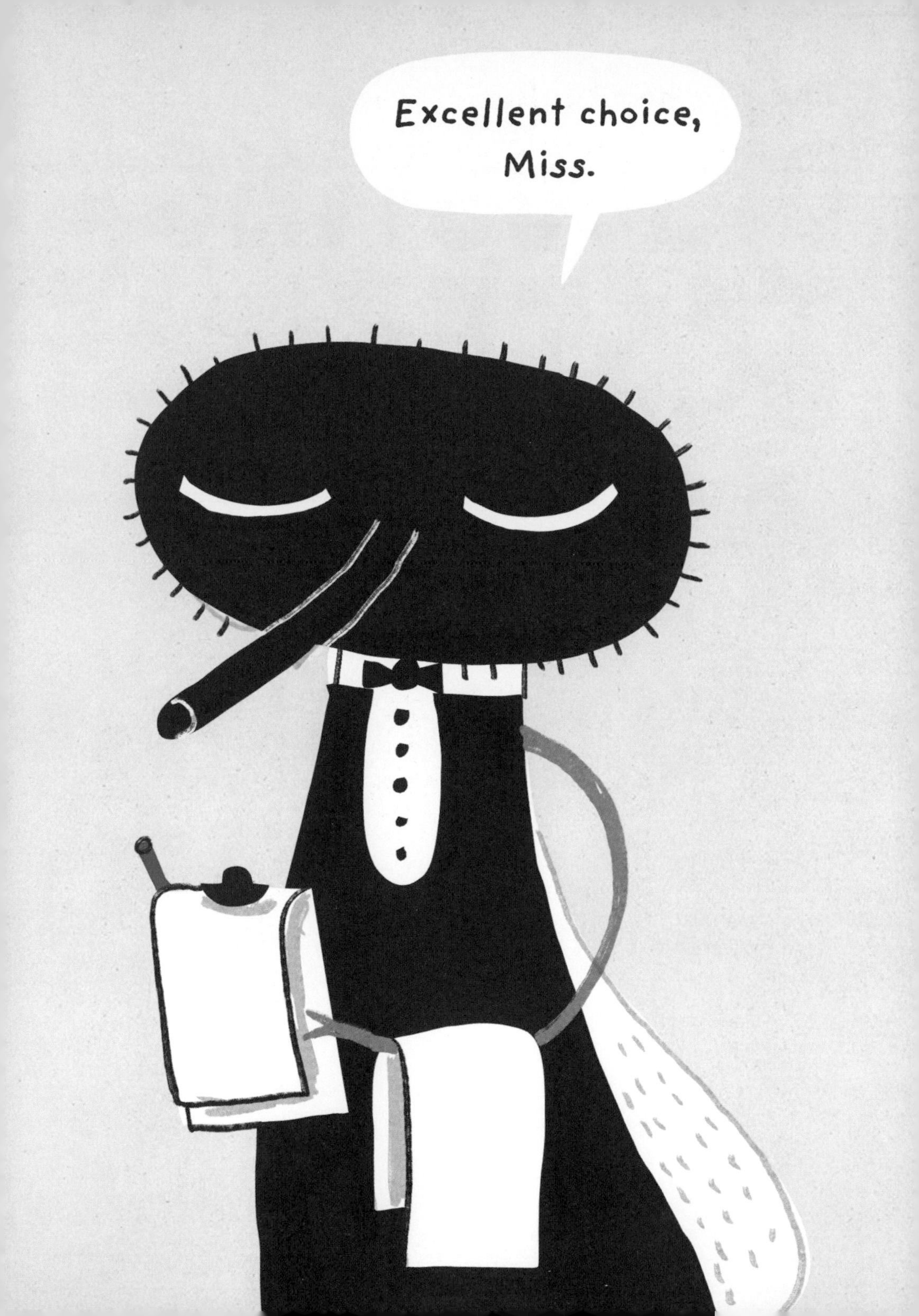
Excellent choice, Miss.

The female fly can lay over a hundred eggs at a time. From the egg comes a maggot, which then turns into a pupa, which then becomes a fly.

MAGGOT

PUPA

FLY

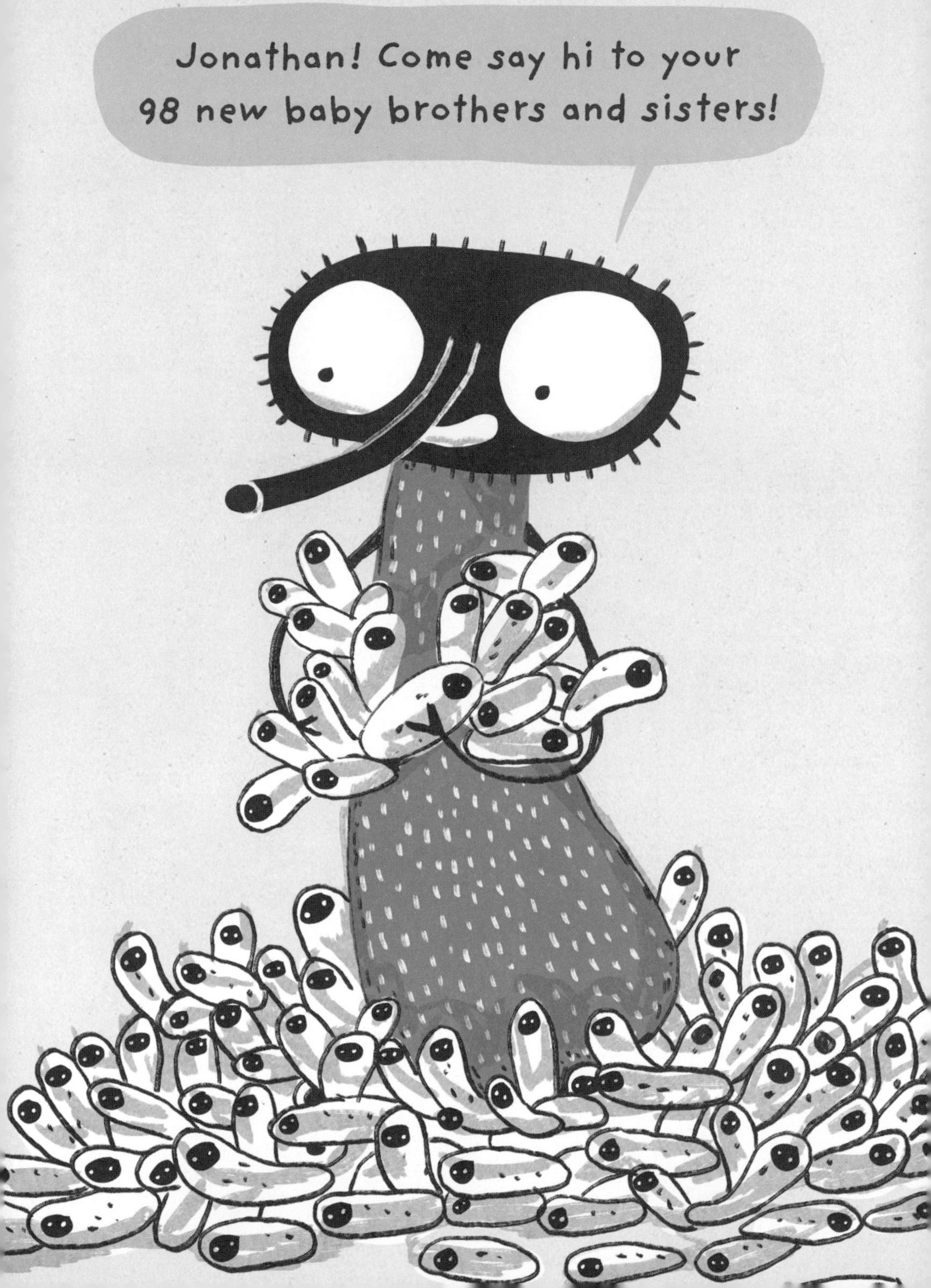
Jonathan! Come say hi to your 98 new baby brothers and sisters!

The fly can be eaten by other insects, such as spiders, or by birds or fish. The fly lives between

15 AND 30 DAYS.

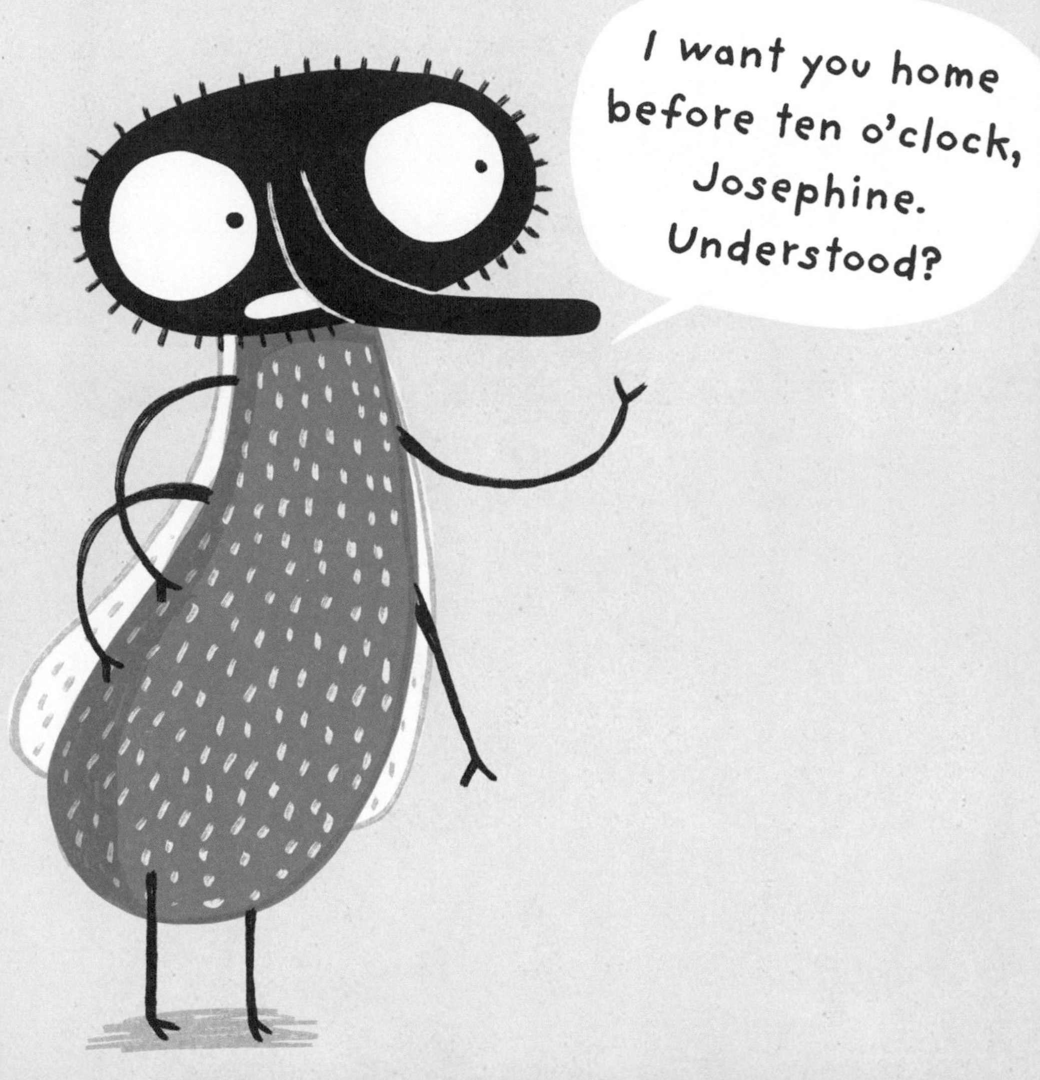
I want you home before ten o'clock, Josephine. Understood?

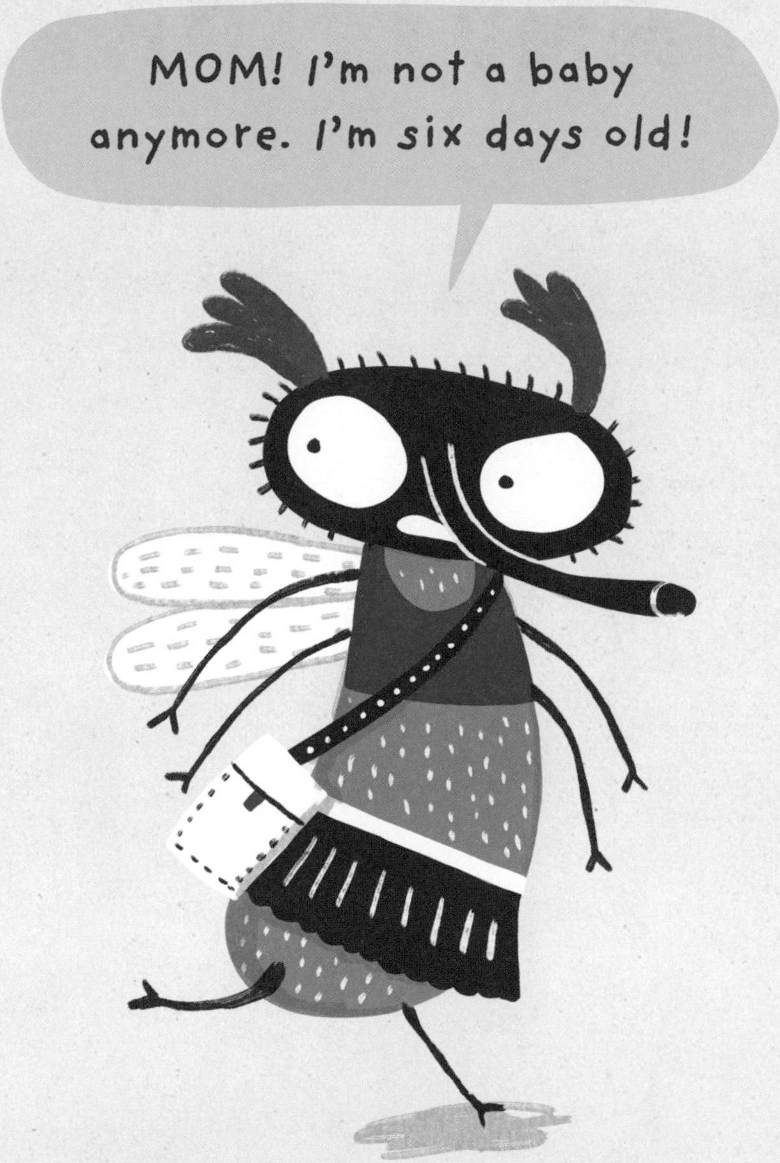
MOM! I'm not a baby anymore. I'm six days old!

Because he walks on garbage and gross stuff like poo, the fly can carry

GERMS

and cause hundreds of

DISEASES.

Good morning.
You ordered a flu?

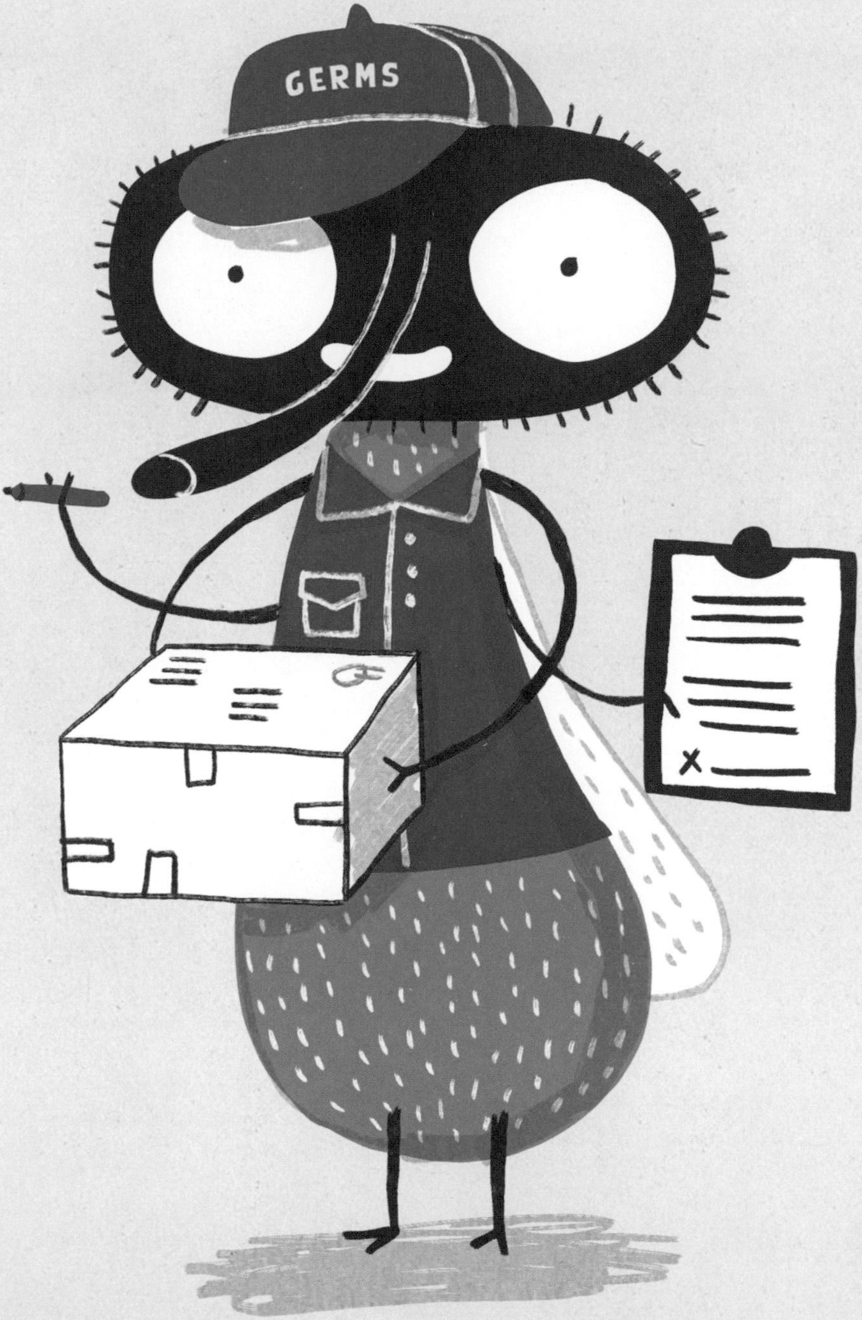
GERMS

So next time a fly wants to share your food, make sure he washes

HIS HANDS.

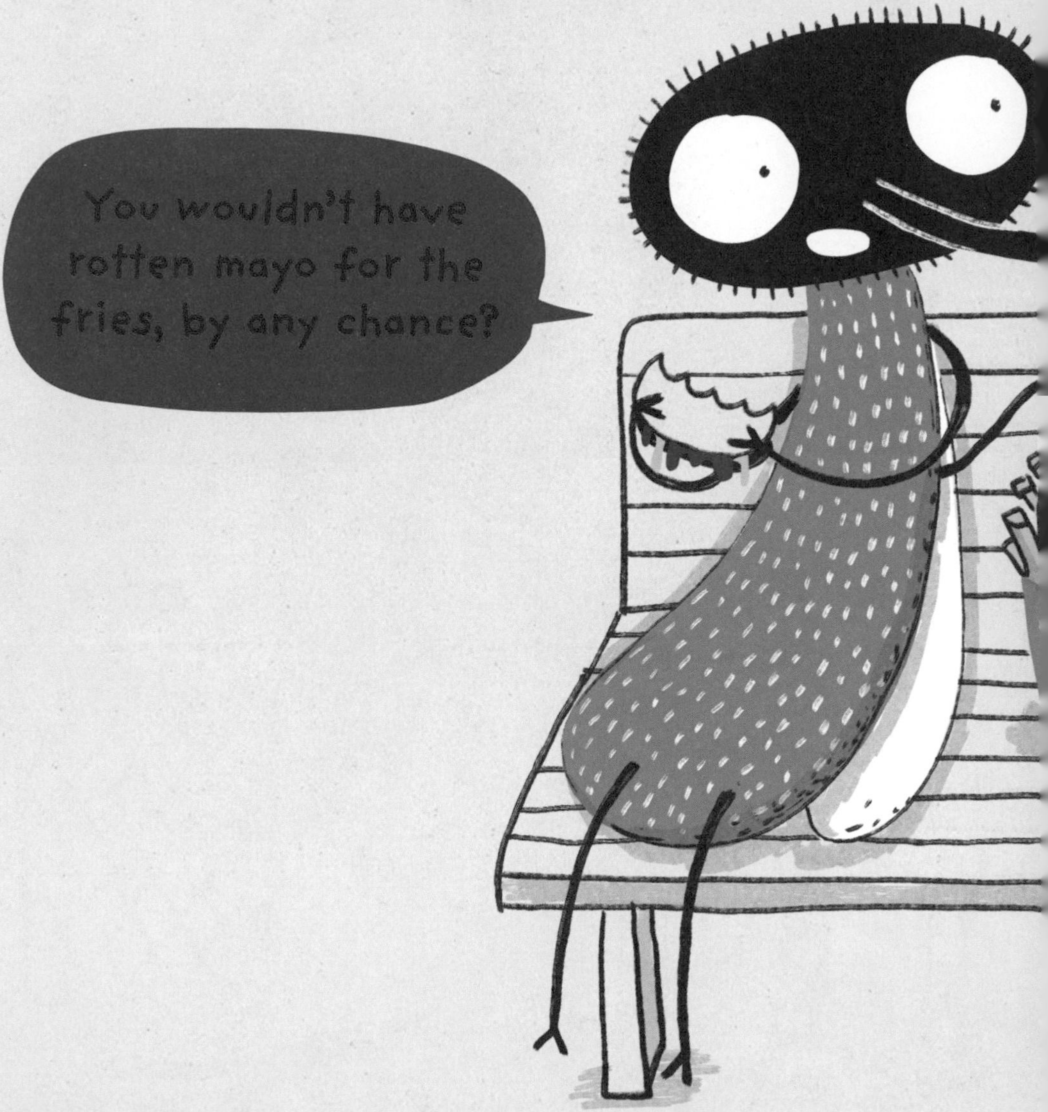
You wouldn't have rotten mayo for the fries, by any chance?

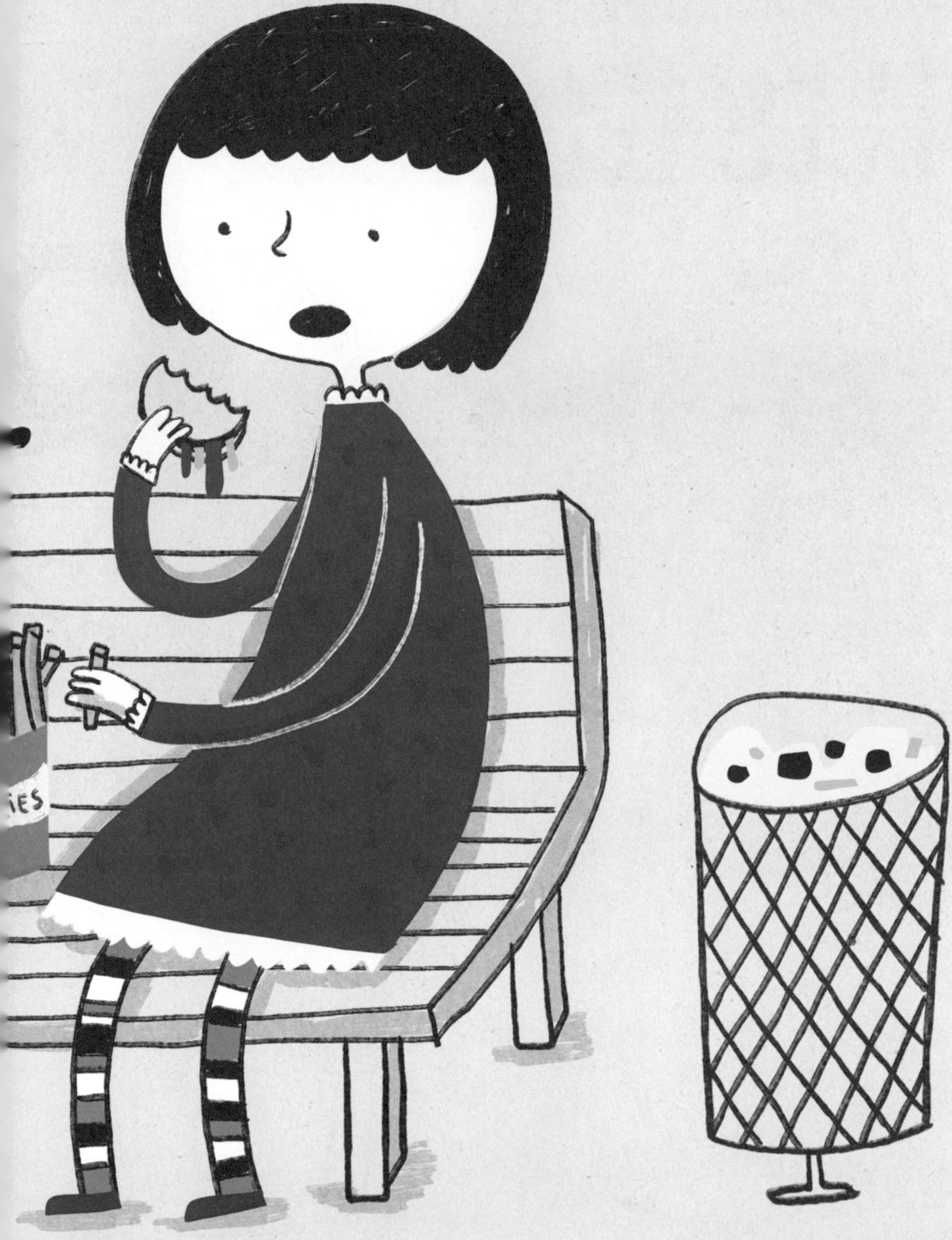

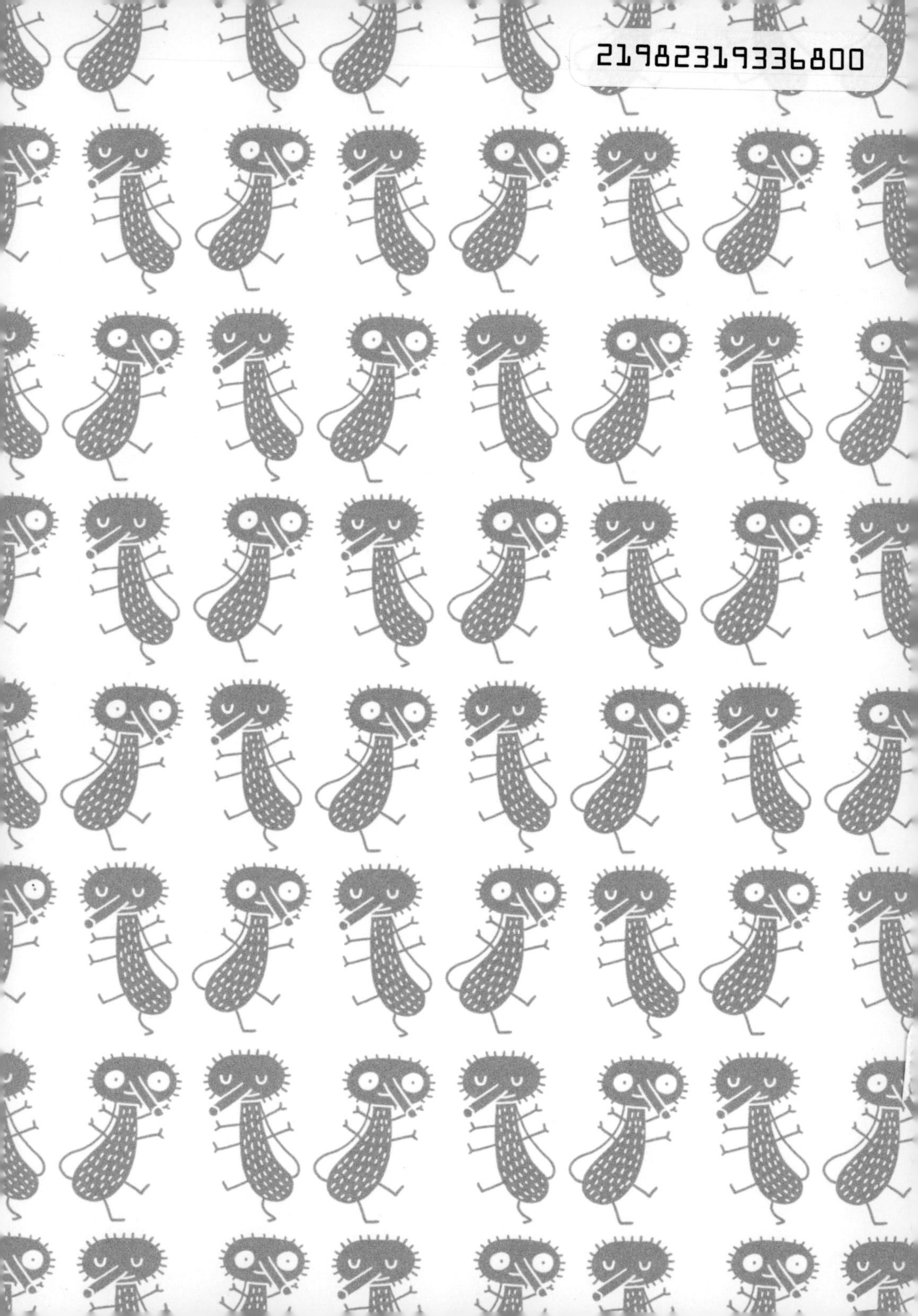